Praise for
Frog and Toad are Doing Their Best

"This book is hilarious, and I also want to wear it
like a cozy, friendly sweater."

—Emily Flake,
New Yorker cartoonist and author of
That Was Awkward: The Art and Etiquette of the Awkward Hug

"This book is like a cup of chamomile at bedtime, but one that makes you
laugh out loud and feel soothed and understood. So, I really recommend
picking up this rather than a cup of tea."

—Julie Vick,
author of *Babies Don't Make Small Talk (So Why Should I?)*

"If you like to laugh, this book is for you. If you like nostalgia, this book
is for you. If you want coziness, this book is for you. If you don't like any
of those things, may I recommend a rusty nail to the thigh?"

—Johnathan Appel,
writer for *Last Week Tonight with John Oliver*

"In these unprecedented times, it makes sense that we would turn to
the classic characters of Frog and Toad for laughs, joy, and the soothing
pleasures of two amphibians who love to be friends. I've scream-laughed
at and obsessively shared Jennie's amazing short pieces, and this book is
a perfect vehicle to reintroduce these characters to a modern context."

—Caitlin Kunkel,
co-author of *New Erotica for Feminists* and
co-founder of The Satire and Humor Festival

"Jennie's book reminds us that while most millennials do not live in a pastoral fairy-tale lily pad, it is always better to approach our 21st-Century problems like timeless, whimsical, clothed amphibians: with humor, honesty, and with a generous dose of kindness toward others and ourselves."

—Felipe Torres Medina,
writer for *The Late Show with Stephen Colbert*

"I laughed, I cried, I felt hopeful and mad and tired and seen. But mostly I felt jealous because who writes this well all the time?"

—Brooke Preston,
co-author of *New Erotica for Feminists*
and co-founder of The Belladonna

"From dealing with crappy Wi-Fi to wanting everyone to like you, this modern take on a truly great classic had us laughing out loud. We've never related more to our favorite amphibian duo! *Frog and Toad are Doing Their Best* is just the laugh we need these days."

—Laura Lane and Ellen Haun,
authors of *Cinderella and the Glass Ceiling:
And Other Feminist Fairy Tales*

"This book will be famous, so I'm glad my name is on it."

—Elissa Bassist,
editor of the Funny Women column on *The Rumpus*

Oh, Bother

Winnie-the-Pooh is Befuddled, Too

....

(A Smackerel-Sized Parody
of Modern Life)

by Jennie Egerdie
Illustrated by Ellie Hajdu

RUNNING PRESS
PHILADELPHIA

Running Press
Hachette Book Group
1290 Avenue of the Americas, New York, NY 10104
www.runningpress.com
@Running_Press

First Edition: May 2024

Published by Running Press, an imprint of Hachette Book Group, Inc.
The Running Press name and logo are trademarks of Hachette Book Group, Inc.

The Hachette Speakers Bureau provides a wide range of authors for speaking events.
To find out more, go to www.hachettespeakersbureau.com
or email HachetteSpeakers@hbgusa.com.

Running Press books may be purchased in bulk for business,
educational, or promotional use. For more information, please contact your
local bookseller or the Hachette Book Group Special Markets Department
at Special.Markets@hbgusa.com.

The publisher is not responsible for websites (or their content)
that are not owned by the publisher.

Print book cover and interior design by Frances J. Soo Ping Chow.

Library of Congress Cataloging-in-Publication Data
Names: Egerdie, Jennie, author. | Hajdu, Ellie, illustrator.
Title: Oh, bother : Winnie-the-Pooh is befuddled, too (a smackerel-sized parody
of modern life) / by Jennie Egerdie; illustrated by Ellie Hajdu.
Description: First edition. | Philadelphia : Running Press, 2024. |
Identifiers: LCCN 2023040212 | ISBN 9780762486274 (hardcover) |
ISBN 9780762486281 (ebook)
Subjects: LCSH: Milne, A. A. (Alan Alexander), 1882-1956—Parodies,
imitations, etc. | Conduct of life—Humor | Life skills—Humor. |
LCGFT: Parodies (Literature) | Humor.
Classification: LCC PN6231.P3 E36 2024 | DDC 818/.607—dc23/eng/20230911
LC record available at https://lccn.loc.gov/2023040212

ISBNs: 978-0-7624-8627-4 (hardcover), 978-0-7624-8628-1 (ebook)

Printed in the United States of America

LSC-C

Printing 1, 2024

Contents

How to Play Pooh Sticks

Pooh Sticks is played with two or more players,
or by yourself with the river.

1. Select a stick. (Any stick will do, but
   preferably one that feels nice in your hand.)
2. Stand in the middle of a bridge facing upstream.
3. Hold your stick out at arm's length over the stream.
4. On the count of three, drop your stick
   into the water together with any other players.
5. Turn to the downstream side of the bridge.
6. Wait for the sticks to float by.
7. The first stick to float from under the bridge is
   the winner.

BEE
TREE

BIG
STONES
AND
ROX

RISING RIVER

100 AKER
WOOD

DR. FESTINKER'S
OFFICE

OWL'S
HOUSE

EEYORE'S
GLOOMY
PLACE

To my brave friend Piglet,
or Molly, as she's known

Author's Note

———∿∿∿∿∿∿———

I DON'T KNOW what's going to happen in the future, but I know what I'll do tonight: Lie on my couch, stare at the ceiling, and worry about everything that's out of my control.

What if my mom gets sick? What if rising sea levels swallow my apartment? What if I'm maimed by a falling pile of space garbage and my insurance doesn't cover it?

Just when I'm about to throw up with panic, I remember a chubby little buddy who lives completely in the moment. I take a deep breath and ask myself: *What would Pooh do?*

It's been a hundred years since A. A. Milne's *Winnie-the-Pooh* was first published, filling our hearts with sweet adventures and funny misunderstandings. Yet even in that idyllic childhood setting, Milne's Hundred Acre Wood was never perfect. Bears were stuck, tails got lost, and homes flooded with rain. Despite all this chaos, stories ended happily because the characters looked out for each other.

The world has changed since we first met Pooh. Our challenges are different. But the need for friendship remains the same. I need my community, just as Pooh needs Piglet's deep kindness, Rabbit's sharp practicality, Owl's well-intentioned wisdom, Tigger's exuberance, Eeyore's righteous melancholy, and the warmth of Kanga and Roo. These days, we're all a little lost in the (Hundred Acre) woods. But with help from Pooh and Piglet, we can make it home together.

*"Supposing a tree fell down, Pooh,
when we were underneath it?"*

*"Supposing it didn't," said Pooh
after careful thought.*

Piglet was comforted by this.

—*The House at Pooh Corner,*
A. A. Milne

In Which Pooh Feels
Anxious about the Bees

O NE DAY IN the Hundred Acre Wood—

Actually, no one was sure if the wood was a hundred acres or not, what with all the encroaching big-box stores. Suffice to say, there was still a great deal of woods in the wood, though the exact distance hadn't been measured in a very long time—

"Pardon me," said Winnie-the-Pooh. "But does this have anything to do with the story?"

No, not a bit.

"Then, shall we . . ." gestured Pooh kindly with a sticky paw, "begin?"

On this bright day, sitting high on a branch of the honey tree, Winnie-the-Pooh carefully stuck his arm into the trunk, feeling around for a swatch of sticky goodness.

"Mmm, mmm, mmm," hummed Pooh, bouncing a happy honey bounce as he ate. He stuck his paw in for another lick.

And another.

And another.

As he helped himself to fistfuls of honey, Pooh expected to feel the familiar (and unpleasant) sting of a bee. But today no sting came.

"That's strange," said Pooh to himself. "Usually, the bees buzz about, being very bothersome with their stingers." Pooh smiled. "Perhaps I should thank the bees for their kindness."

Pooh knocked politely on the trunk of the tree. "Hello, bees?" He called out, "It's me, Winnie-the-Pooh." Hearing no answer, Pooh stuck his head inside the tree. He saw a few tired-looking, very sweaty bees packing tiny troves of honey.

"Oh," said Pooh. "There are a lot fewer bees than there were before. Less honey too." Pooh continued snacking, his paws dripping with amber goo.

But after a few minutes of contented snacking, Pooh thought of Something Important, a Something that did not make him happy at all. "Fewer bees," gasped Pooh, "means less HONEY."

Pooh went pale.

What if ALL the bees went away? Pooh hastily reached for another comforting smackeral. "I mustn't worry on an empty stomach," Pooh told himself, patting his round tummy, which was groaning with each additional mouthful. "I'll just eat one more bite—then maybe one more after that—until I feel better."

Pooh ate, and ate, and ate, putting all his worry into each mouthful until, finally, he was too stuffed to think anything at all. Which is just the way he liked it.

Once Winnie-the-Pooh recovered from his honey-coma, he went looking for answers in the most knowledgeable place he could think of.

Pooh knocked on Owl's door. "Hullo? Owl?"

Pooh heard some rustling, then the door opened. "Why, it's Pooh Bear!" Owl exclaimed. "How're things, my dear friend?"

"Not very well," admitted Pooh, "I wonder if you know about bees? And honey?"

Pooh launched into his tale of the strange happenings at the honey tree.

"Bees! Gone missing? How unusual!" declared Owl. "You know, I had a Great-Uncle Polonius who was one for apiology—that is, of course, the scientifical study of honeybees—"

"Did you say honey?" asked Pooh. Pooh felt worried again, which made his tummy extra rumbly. A little snack might ease his mind.

"Oh, yes, do help yourself," said Owl, ushering Pooh towards his table, which was set for afternoon tea. "Now, what was I saying?"

"You were thpeaking about Uncle Ponybuth," said Pooh thickly, struggling through a mouthful of honey.

"Ah yes," said Owl. "Great-Uncle Polonius was a bird for the bees. In fact, when one speaks of 'the birds and the bees,' this is a shorthand for my great-uncle's research. Why, it was he who discovered the negative effect of pesky-sides—"

"Pardon me," said Pooh, "but what are pesky . . . sides?"

"My dear Pooh," said Owl loftily, "everybody knows a pesky-side is a thing that stops bees and bugs from doing the things that bees and bugs do."

"Who would want that?" asked Pooh, holding up a sticky paw in surprise.

"Oh, it was the fashion some time ago," said Owl, flapping his wings comfortingly.

"But, some time ago is not now," said Pooh, confused. "So does that mean the bees are fine?"

"Not at all!" said Owl cheerfully. "It isn't only the pesky-sides that put the bees and bugs in grave danger. There is also the warming of the weather, the change in flora . . . Of course, if you were to read my great-uncle's histories—"

But Pooh couldn't hear Owl anymore. The bees? In danger? From someone named Flora?

Pooh felt frightened, which felt just like being worried, which meant he had the strong urge to eat. He dunked his paw into the mostly empty honey pot, careful to reach about for every last bit of sweetness before licking his paws clean. He then made quick work of the condensed milk. And the toast. And the biscuits. Every bite made him feel a little bit better and a little bit worse.

Soon, Owl's table was completely empty.

"Is there any more?" asked Pooh, holding his sore tummy.

"Pooh!" said Owl gravely. "You can't still be hungry?"

"Oh, no, I'm quite full," admitted Pooh. "But you see, in times like this, I could always use a little more."

❧ ☙

Pooh lay on the ground of his thoughtful spot, rubbing his bloated, swollen tummy. He felt sick. And terrible. And worst of all, he couldn't eat anything else to stop his mind from whirling because there was no more room in his tummy. He let out a very big sigh.

"What's wrong, Pooh Bear?" asked Christopher Robin.

"Everything," grumbled Pooh.

Christopher Robin looked affectionately at his tubby friend as he pulled a pink bottle out of his backpack. He opened the bottle and gave Pooh two spoonfuls to soothe his stomach.

After a few minutes of sighing and rubbing his belly, Pooh sat up.

"I could not stop my mind from thinking," said Pooh, "which is to say, I could not stop my mouth from eating.

It seems my mind and my mouth have more space than my tummy."

"What are you thinking about, Pooh?" asked Christopher Robin.

"I am thinking that there may be no more bees someday, and if there are no more bees, there will be no more honey," shuddered Pooh, clutching his stomach tightly for comfort.

"So you ate until there was no more honey today?" said Christopher Robin. "Silly old bear!"

"It seemed like a good idea at the time," sighed Pooh. "Christopher Robin? I am not a bear for all this thinking. Which is to say, I am not a bear for thinking at all. What do you do when you can't stop worrying?"

"I haven't thought about that," answered Christopher Robin slowly. "I suppose instead of thinking about what I'm scared of, I try to think about things that are good. Like you."

"I shall try that," said Pooh with a yawn. He was feeling quite sleepy now that his tummy had settled a bit. "I will do just that—right after a nap."

In Which Eeyore Goes to Therapy:
SESSION 1

———∿∿∿∿∿∿∿∿∿———

DEEP IN THE Hundred Acre Wood, in a
sensibly furnished den, Eeyore shared feelings of
inadequacy with his therapist, Dr. Festinker.

"Everyone in the Hundred Acre Wood has a home," he
complained, "and I live in a wobbly tent of sticks."

"I'm sorry," said Dr. Festinker. "That must feel terrible."

Eeyore shook his head from side to side. "Not much use
feeling bad about it," sighed Eeyore. "Feeling bad doesn't
build me a house."

"Maybe not," agreed Dr. Festinker. "But ignoring your
feelings will only lead to resentment and make it harder for
you to make the changes you desire in your life."

Eeyore stared at his skunk therapist. He took in her deep,
sympathetic gaze as well as her strong, pungent scent. (This
was the reason behind her very reasonable rates: a sliding
scale based on each patient's tolerance of the odor.)

Eeyore let out a long, slow sigh. "Can't help noticing you're right."

"Have you told your friends how you feel about your home?" asked Dr. Festinker.

"No," said Eeyore.

"What do you think would happen if you asked for their help in finding you a home like theirs?" encouraged the skunk.

"I think they would help me," admitted Eeyore glumly.

Dr. Festinker smiled.

"Not that they think of me as a friend," added Eeyore. "They only keep me around so they have someone to blame when it rains."

In Which Owl Is Very Online

~~~~~~~~~~~~~~~~

ONE AFTERNOON AS Owl was flying above the wood, he spotted a battered laptop lying in the middle of the dandelion meadow. After inquiring around if anyone had misplaced it, Owl tentatively opened the laptop. Being an intellectual fowl with a great deal of free time, Owl quickly found the computer to be magnificent company and used the machine daily to expand his, and others', knowledge.

Every night after dinner, Owl would turn on his favorite podcast, "Owl Things Considered," and log in to Wikipedia to correct misinformation about Owls.

"Owls are birds . . . yes, that's right," nodded Owl to himself. "They are divided into two families . . . hogwash!" Owl laughed as he clicked the edit button. "A-l-l owls are part of one large and rather illustrious family tree. The most famous owl is my great-great-great-uncle Strigidae the Magic, noted companion of the wizard Merlin, and author of the grimoire Calendarium Featherale Magicum Plumagetuum." Owl slowly typed in the name of his grand relation's book; correcting the history of the owl family meant a great deal to him.

"Now what do we have here . . . 'Owls are carnivorous and live on diets of insects, small rodents . . .' Absolutely not." He chortled as he deleted the entry. "Owls eat a great deal of things," he typed. "Mostly bread, condensed milk, and in the summer months, my Great-Uncle Emeril's delicious peachseed cobbler."

"Great-Uncle Emeril," added Owl, "was also the uncredited creator of the Little Debbie cake." At this remembrance, Owl got up to grab a small snack cake from his kitchen before continuing his important work.

"What else, what else," said Owl to himself, munching the teeny cake happily as he read on. "Why, it says, 'Female owls stay at their nest with their eggs.' True, but terribly incomplete." Owl clucked his beak disapprovingly. "Everyone knows my Great-Aunt Ermengarde once laid a seagull egg by mistake. Luckily," he added, "she was very fond of the sea, and didn't mind her offspring in the slightest."

At this time, Owl was feeling quite fussy. All the incorrect information made him utterly overwhelmed.

"I say, that's enough for one night," sputtered Owl. He switched tabs to join in an online discussion about how the earth is, in truth, flat. "It's as if they're deliberately trying to spread falsehoods! Why, it makes it impossible to believe anything you read online."

In Which Our Friends Meet
an Incredulous Marmot

~~~~~~~~~~~~~~~~~~

NOBODY SEEMED TO know why the river was so high that year, but it was certainly higher than before. Everyone in the Hundred Acre Wood had learned to be cautious about floods and crumbling riverbanks during the rainy season, which is when this story takes place.

Pooh, Piglet, and Eeyore were walking in their rainy-day hats and slickers, following the river along its path to the wooden bridge where they aimed to play a few rounds of Pooh Sticks.

"Oh!" Piglet gave a little squeak of excitement. "Do you think the river will-will-will flood?"

"It may," said Pooh, after a minute of careful thinking. "But I am a Pooh Bear, not a river. So I do not know what a river will do."

"It'll flood," remarked Eeyore gloomily, "At least, when it does, I won't need a bath."

Suddenly Pooh saw something Very Interesting.

"Look!" Pooh pointed to a curious pair of ears poking out from the ground near the riverbed.

"Perhaps we should see who those ears belong to," said Pooh. "Maybe someone lost them."

"I d-d-don't like it," shivered Piglet. "Ears on the g-g-ground all willy-nilly . . ."

"I'll stay here," said Eeyore, taking a seat on the muddy path. "That way, when everything goes wrong, I can call for help."

As Piglet and Pooh approached the river, it became very clear the ears were not on the ground all willy-nilly. They were attached to a rather large marmot sitting in a rocking chair in a sizable hole that was quickly filling up with water.

"Oh!" cried Piglet. "Do you need help?"

"With what?" said the marmot.

"With the water?" said Pooh. "You're sitting in it."

"Nope," said the marmot. "No water here."

"But it is," said Piglet confusedly. "The river's flooding."

"Absolutely not," said the marmot, who was now quite submerged from the waist down. "I've lived here all my life, and the river's way over thataway. Always has been, always will be. There's no water here."

And with that, the marmot continued to rock back and forth as the water rose slowly around him. He reached down and took a sip from a teacup floating along on its saucer.

Flummoxed, Piglet and Pooh wandered back towards Eeyore, who was having a conversation with a lady marmot holding a sensible umbrella. She wore a disgusted look on her face.

"Don't pay any attention to him," said the lady marmot. "He's stubborn, that one. My Uncle Fergus, he is. While the rest of us evacuated our homes for a burrow higher up once the river started rising, he refuses to believe anything changes. Just sits in that puddle of a house, he does, waiting to turn into a frog."

"Which he won't, of course," clarified Eeyore, once he saw Pooh's puzzled look.

"B-b-but," stuttered Piglet, his face filled with worry. "His home!"

"We've told him, and told him, but you know the type. Some folks won't admit the sky is blue until it crashes down on 'em. There's nothing to be done," said the lady marmot, patting Piglet's hand kindly. "You just go about your business, now, and leave Fergus to the water. If you ask me, a good soaking might wash the nonsense out of him."

With that, she hurried along the path towards a small spinney of larch trees on a nearby hill.

So Pooh, Piglet, and Eeyore walked a little farther down the path until they came upon the bridge to play Pooh Sticks. After a few rounds of play (at which Pooh won once, Piglet twice, and Eeyore not at all) the rain changed from a pleasant drip-dripping into a more serious plop-plop-plopping, and then started pouring down much harder than before. They agreed to play one more round just as Eeyore spotted a rather large, fuzzy animal in a rocking chair floating toward them.

"I'm probably wrong," moaned Eeyore, "but isn't that the marmot who lives up the river?"

"I don't know," said Pooh, eyes wide. "This marmot is an awful lot soggier than the other marmot."

They did not have to wait long, for rain and river picked up their pace and the fuzzy wet rocking animal drifted close by.

"Hullo there!" called Pooh.

"Hullo," said Fergus.

"Are you in need of some assist-, asissystance?" said Pooh.

"Absolutely—NOT!" cried Fergus, desperately trying to keep his head above water. "And you three busybodies better stay off my proper—" he couldn't finish his sentence, for a small wave had filled his mouth with water.

"Well," remarked Eeyore. "It is him." With that, he turned and began to plod his way down to the edge of the river.

Piglet began walking in small, worried circles. "I don't know, I don't know," said Piglet anxiously, wringing his small pink trotters. "I don't know what to d-d-do! He doesn't want help, but it doesn't seem right to leave him in the rain and the water—"

Pooh scratched his head, puzzled by all this. "Perhaps," he said thoughtfully, "sometimes one is in need of asissystance, even when one does not want asissystance."

"But is that the right thing to d-d-do!?" exclaimed Piglet, working himself into a right tizzy. "He did ask us to leave him alone! But being a very small animal myself, I know the deep water is frightening, and maybe he does need our help when he says he doesn't, but—"

"Pooh," called Eeyore. While Piglet and Pooh were discussing the best course of action, he had already begun to wade into the water. "Can you come hold my tail, please?"

"Oh!" said Pooh. "Yes."

So Pooh hurried over to the water's edge and took hold of Eeyore's tail. Piglet, from the bank, held Pooh's back paw to help keep him balanced. Steadied, Eeyore waded farther into the water. Just as the marmot was about to pass, Eeyore caught the back of the now-submerged rocking chair in his mouth.

"Mmmrph!" said Eeyore.

"Pardon?" said Pooh.

"I think he wants you to p-pull him to shore!" squeaked Piglet, trembling with effort.

The three of them moved slowly, dragging the spluttering marmot with them. Soon, they all collapsed in a heap on the water's edge, tired but satisfied.

"That," said Piglet, looking at Eeyore admiringly, "was a very good idea."

The marmot, however, had finished coughing out river water and was eyeing all three with aggravation.

"Good idea?" grumbled Fergus. "Why, I almost drowned! That river's so high, no critter can live by it! Why didn't any of you say something?"

"Excuse me," said Pooh, confused. "But we did tell you, didn't we?"

"Did not!" yelled Fergus, wringing out his fur. "Didn't say one word about water, or danger, and now look at me! All because you three know-nothin' pumpkin-headed numbskulls couldn't be bothered to warn a marmot!"

Piglet stuttered with frustration. Eeyore closed his eyes and counted to three. And Pooh, who had been frowning, rubbed his nose and blinked very firmly, saying nothing at all. At their silence, the marmot threw his paws in the air and stumped off towards higher ground.

"Pathetic," said Eeyore, watching him go. "That's what that is." He rolled his gloomy eyes towards Pooh and Piglet. "And I should know."

"Do you think we made him very mad?" said Piglet, still trembling from the conflict.

"I don't know, Piglet," said Pooh.

"The way I see it, Pooh Bear," sighed Eeyore. "There's just no pleasing some people, and that's all there is to it."

In Which Eeyore Goes to Therapy:

SESSION 17

~~~~~~~~

EYORE WAS REMEMBERING a trauma.

"And then," said Eeyore, "my tail went missing."

"That sounds very hard," said his therapist.

"It was," said Eeyore gloomily. "Have you ever lost a tail?"

"Can't say that I have," said Dr. Festinker.

"That's what I thought," said Eeyore, gazing sadly at his therapist. "Losing a tail is terrible. But it got worse. My tail was at Owl's house being used . . . as a *bell-pull*."

Eeyore let out a long, sad sigh.

"My tail . . ." He moaned, slowly shaking his head. "A doorbell!"

"I'm sorry that happened to you," said Dr. Festinker.

"Owl didn't even *notice* it was my tail," said Eeyore with a great deal of self-pity. "He would have noticed if it were Pooh's tail. Pooh's the best bear in all the world. And what am I? A grey, gloomy donkey, with a droopy tail that keeps getting lost."

"Eeyore, you have many strengths," said Dr. Festinker kindly. "But what if, since losing your tail bothers you so, you left your tail at home?"

"Can't," answered Eeyore.

There was a long silence.

Dr. Festinker politely counted to ten in her head.

In Which Everyone
Tries Their Best at Yoga

〜〜〜〜〜〜〜

A S YOU EXHALE," said Kanga, reaching her paws to the sky. "Bend your knees so that your thighs are as parallel to the floor as possible. This is chair pose."

Tigger, Rabbit, Piglet, and Roo groaned as they strained to hold the position.

"Tiggers do not like chair pose," muttered Tigger crossly.

"Am I doing this right?" asked Piglet, wobbling on the tips of his trotters.

"Not quite, Piglet," said Kanga kindly. "Plant your heels flat on the ground, and try to lower your center of gravity just a bit more."

Piglet adjusted his body, his pink face growing even pinker with effort.

"What about this!" said Tigger, bouncing forward onto his front paws and wagging his legs in the sky. "What's this called?"

"A handstand," answered Kanga. "But that's not what we're aiming for right now—"

"I want to try!" said Roo eagerly, bouncing around his mat in circles.

"Kanga?" called Rabbit, pointing to the back of the meadow. "Pooh's doing yoga wrong."

Pooh was lying on his back, napping soundly. He sighed and smiled in his sleep.

"Pooh's doing very well," nodded Kanga. "That's called a restorative yoga practice."

TWUMP

Tigger tumbled to the ground, making a noise between a growl and a yelp.

"Ouch!" said Tigger, rubbing his tail. "Yoga is *not* what Tiggers like best."

In Which Rabbit Gardens and
Pooh Discovers a New Room

~~~~~~~~~~~~~

R ABBIT WOKE UP with a start. He had that
funny, bunny feeling again, the one that says
"Take charge," and "You're the captain," and
especially "Everything and everyone depends on you!" So

after meticulously scrubbing down his kitchen (part of his patented post-breakfast routine) Rabbit sniffed the early summer air and knew exactly what to do.

"Today, like every day," he said to himself, "I must tend to my garden."

Rabbit's garden was originally a small, tidy plot in front of his home. Tending his plants gave Rabbit a great sense of purpose. But the past few years of warmer weather and odd storms had made gardening tougher, and he started to get a queasy feeling in his stomach.

"What if, next year, it rains all summer?" He worried at night, tossing and turning in his bed.

"Or the soil is too dry? What if the plants don't grow? What then?"

So Rabbit expanded his garden from one small plot into sixteen neat rows of vegetables that spanned the entire open space in front of his burrow. He spent morning, noon, and night tending to the vegetables and obsessing over all the things he couldn't control. "If I just keep working," thought Rabbit nervously, "surely things will be fine."

On this early summer morning, Rabbit was busy digging small holes in the garden as Pooh walked by, humming gently to himself.

"Hullo, Rabbit," said Pooh.

"Pooh Bear!" said Rabbit, jumping with alarm. "Don't you sneak up on me like that!"

"I shall try not to," said Pooh solemnly. "What are you doing?"

"Me?" said Rabbit. "What does it look like I'm doing?"

"Digging holes," answered Pooh.

"Yes, yes, quite right," answered Rabbit. "I'm planting rutabaga seedlings."

"Oh yes," said Pooh. "And what, Rabbit, do those say?" Pooh pointed to three signs surrounding the plot, which said "GO AWY," "KEAP OOT," and "NO BUNCING."

"Those signs are for Tigger," explained Rabbit as he watered his newly homed rutabagas. "Last week he and Roo came by and nearly bounced my potatoes out of the ground!"

"It does seem like you have an awful lot of potatoes," said Pooh, staring at a huge thicket of plants.

"Not enough," grimaced Rabbit. He put down his shovel and cracked his back. It was nearing eleven in the morning, and eleven is the time for a smackerel. "Pooh, would you like to come in for a snack?"

"Why, yes, Rabbit," smiled Pooh. "I was hoping you would say that."

Pooh followed Rabbit through the garden, past the many rain barrels along the sandy banks of his home, and inside the burrow. As Rabbit went to get plates and mugs, Pooh stood in the entrance, his eyes adjusting to the light.

"Rabbit," said Pooh. "What is that?" Pooh pointed to a very large, very round container sitting next to the cupboard. It was so large it almost touched the roof.

"Oh, that," said Rabbit proudly, "is a tank of emergency potable water I keep in my home at all times."

"You can make water out of potatoes?" asked a confused Pooh.

"Not potatoes, *potable*. This is extra drinking water."

"But why, Rabbit?"

"One can never have too much water," said Rabbit as he placed honey, condensed milk, and brown bread on the table. "And it helps me feel less nervous."

Pooh nodded in an understanding sort of way. He sat at the table where a great many seeds were sorted into piles. "One, two, three," counted Pooh.

"Oh, don't touch, don't touch," said Rabbit, rushing over to protect the deliberate piles he had spent all yesterday sorting. "These are my heirloom seeds."

"Do you need so many?" asked Pooh, as his paw itched towards the honey pot.

"Well, no," admitted Rabbit. "But, you see, there's enough seeds here for acres of garden, for miles of garden, for gardens for many years!"

"That's an awful lot of garden," said Pooh. "Do you want that much garden, Rabbit?"

"It's not about *wanting* a large garden," sniffed Rabbit. "The point is to have seeds, just in case."

"In case of what?" asked Pooh.

"In case anything happens," said Rabbit.

"But Rabbit," laughed Pooh, "things happen all the time."

"Exactly," nodded Rabbit.

Pooh said nothing, as he was quite confused and more than a little hungry. But after a few pawfuls, Rabbit's honey pot was bare, and Pooh's tummy soon rumbled rather threateningly.

"Rabbit," asked Pooh. "Is there any more?"

"I have some extra in the cellar," said Rabbit vaguely.

"A cellar!" said Pooh, quite surprised. "I didn't know you had a cellar."

"It's new," said Rabbit, as he hopped quickly down five rather steep stairs by the back door. "I dug it out last autumn. But—Pooh! Don't come down here!"

Too late. At the promise of honey, Pooh followed Rabbit down the stairs. What he saw gave him quite a shock.

Rabbit had built a cavernous cellar filled to the brim with pickled vegetables, dehydrated beans, jams, squashes, and stacks and stacks of honey pots. Pooh had never seen so much food before, and it struck him so silly he sat right down on the bottom step.

Rabbit hurried over to the honey wall and plucked a single, small pot.

"This should be enough," he said briskly.

"Rabbit," said Pooh, stunned by this new discovery in his very good friend's home. He reached towards the closest shelf to investigate. "What are these? Perhaps we should try a few of these pickled somethings as well—"

"What are you DOING!" exclaimed Rabbit, grabbing the jar of pickled beans from Pooh. "This food is not for eating!"

"But, Rabbit," said Pooh humbly. "I thought all food was for eating."

"It's for eating, but not for eating now—for later!" said Rabbit. "For emergencies!"

"It is an emergency," explained Pooh. "I'm very hungry."

"Well, stop it." huffed Rabbit. "This is for disasters. When a disaster happens, you'll be a lot hungrier then."

"Not if I eat now," whispered Pooh.

"Oh Pooh," groaned Rabbit. "You don't understand."

"But why, Rabbit?" asked Pooh.

"Because no one plans for emergencies!" exploded Rabbit, whose fears had been building up for some time. "What if the worst happens? What will we do? Everyone will say, 'Rabbit, what do we do?' And the best way to make sure nothing happens is to prepare for everything happening—to everyone—all the time. That's why there's enough food here to feed all our friends for . . ." Rabbit counted on his paws, "ten years. Is that enough?" Rabbit started pulling anxiously at his ears.

"Oh Rabbit," said Pooh, patting Rabbit's arm with a sticky paw. "That is a very kind thought. But, does anyone else know about . . . this?"

⟫⟫⟩ ⟨⟨⟨⟵

"Oh my," exhaled Kanga.

"Uh-oh," said Eeyore.

"Oh, d-d-d-dear," stuttered Piglet.

Tigger bounced from aisle to aisle, looking at the piles of food. "Good going, bunny! We'll have a big meal to end all meals, oh boy yessir."

Rabbit hopped from leg to leg nervously. "It's a sensible thing to do," he said rather crossly.

"Yes, dear," said Kanga soothingly. "But it is an awfully large amount."

"No it's not," said Rabbit stubbornly. "Well . . . maybe. Maybe I saved a little more than we need."

"A little!" laughed Tigger, falling onto his back with the giggles. "I'd like to see you try to eat it all!!"

"I wasn't just saving it for me. I wanted to make sure there was enough food for everyone so all of us would be safe forever," admitted Rabbit, realizing as soon as he said it out loud how silly that sounded.

"How nice," groaned Eeyore. "But I don't see any thistles in here for me."

Rabbit pointed to a shady corner with a basket of thistles.

"Never mind," said Eeyore.

"It's a lovely idea," said Kanga carefully. "But maybe this has more to do with worry than food?"

"What if we all helped with your garden, Rabbit?" suggested Piglet. "Then we can each take home the extras so nothing goes to waste?"

"I'll still want to have some stored," warned Rabbit.

"Of course," said Kanga. "But you needn't feel you have to take care of us. We want to take care of you, too."

So Rabbit relaxed a little and opened up his garden to his friends. Every Tuesday, Piglet, Pooh, Tigger, Kanga, and Roo spent the morning weeding and watering—under Rabbit's careful supervision. Come harvest time, everyone pitched in and took a plentiful share home. Soon, all their cupboards were full and nothing went to waste.

But Rabbit still kept a secret stash of safety food in the back of his cellar, next to a few dozen extra jars of his very favorite pickled carrots. Just in case.

"After all," said Rabbit to himself, "you never know when you're going to need it."

In Which Eeyore
Takes a Forest Bath

~~~~~~~~~~~~~~

EYORE SAT QUIETLY among a grove of trees,
breathing deeply. He watched the light dapple
between the leaves of the silver birches. He smelled
the sharp, green scent of the pines and the unfurling bracken
ferns. The early spring of the wood had scattered violets,
buttercups, henbit, and teeny grape hyacinth all around the
grass, nestled in the cool, damp dirt.

Eeyore took long, slow breaths, the kind his therapist had taught him. He drank in the sounds and smells of the forest—the whisper of the wind playing amongst the leaves, the birds chattering, the quiet gurgle of the nearby trickling stream. He felt his body relax.

"I deserve to feel good," Eeyore whispered to himself.

Just then, Tigger bounded into the glade and, not looking where he was bouncing, landed atop Eeyore with the greatest OOPH!

"Hoo-hoo! Didn't see you there, donkey boy!" said Tigger, jumping off of a flat, splayed Eeyore. He lifted the grey donkey and fluffed him back into his usual shape.

"I deserve to . . ." started Eeyore. "Oh, know what, never mind."

In Which Pooh
Sorts His Recycling

———~~~~~———

POOH STOOD IN front of a blue bin and a green
bin. He was holding the pieces of a broken honey
pot he had knocked over that morning.

"Now which . . . goes where?" said Pooh.

A few years ago, the Hundred Acre Wood had started
a recycling program thanks to two of its newest residents:
Heffa and Ronald, a married Heffalump and Woozle. When
they first moved in, Pooh was so afraid for his honey that he

would hide at a mere glance from the pleasant pair. But after some introductions (and after Ronald explained that they were strictly vegan, so did *not* eat honey), Pooh found they were delightful, helpful neighbors. Heffa and Ronald were interested in worm-based composting, weaving rugs from flax, and "clean energy." Pooh didn't understand what any of that meant.

On the blue box was a sign that said, "Metal, glass, plastic, and cartons."

On the green box, "Mixed paper."

Pooh was confused. He had no idea where the pot should go.

"Think, think, think . . ." he said to himself.

Finally, after a few hard minutes of thinking, Pooh carefully placed half of the broken pot in one bin and the rest in the other.

"That's fair," said Pooh pleasantly. "After all, I don't know how to read."

In Which the Day
Is Too Hot

—~~wwwvvvww—

I T WAS A humid summer morning when Pooh and
Piglet sat outside Rabbit's front door listening as Rabbit
listed the varieties of vegetables growing in the August
heat. "There's lettuce, cucumbers, cabbage," Rabbit ticked
off his fingers. "Then there's okra, radishes, summer squash,
beautiful tomatoes . . ."

Pooh struggled to listen. He was preoccupied with
how hot and sticky he felt, especially because feeling sticky
reminded Pooh of honey.

In the distance, a weary-looking trio wandered down
the road, kicking up clouds of dirt as the figures lazily
bounced along. Soon, they were in Rabbit's yard. Tigger
collapsed with an overheated growl at Pooh's feet, while
Piglet passed the thirsty Roo his glass of water.

"Is it really only 7 o'clock in the morning?" asked Kanga,
fanning herself with her paw.

"Yes," said Rabbit somberly. "And the day's only going to get hotter."

"Don't be ridick-orous," said Tigger, jumping up to his feet. "I gotta get goin'! I got a lotta bouncin' to do!"

Tigger bounced one, twice . . . three times in the hot sun before crawling back to the shade of Rabbit's front door.

"Aren't you gonna get bouncing?" asked Roo.

"Uh, sure am," said Tigger, panting on the warm ground. "Just gonna lie down for a bit first, you know, gotta make sure the ground is solid enough for all that jumpin' I'm gonna do."

✿ ✿

That afternoon, the gang sat inside Rabbit's house, the only place in the Hundred Acre Wood with air-conditioning. (Rabbit had harried poor Christopher Robin until he dragged a spare window AC unit from his parents' basement and into the wood for Rabbit.)

The AC cooled the room down only slightly.

"Tiggers do NOT like heat," said Tigger crossly, lying on his stomach underneath Rabbit's kitchen table. "Tiggers

like the cold. We like snow, short days, and ice. The cold is positively what Tiggers love best."

"Mama, I'm bored," complained Roo.

"Me too," sighed Kanga, trying to enjoy the warm breeze blowing from her hand fan. "Does anyone want to play a game?"

"Can't play," said Eeyore, who was chewing on ice and lying under a pile of damp towels. "Can't focus on anything but keeping cool."

"Shh," said Piglet. "You'll wake Pooh."

Pooh was lightly snoring in Rabbit's rocking chair, his toes submerged in a large bucket of cool water.

"He's hoggin' the cool water," growled Tigger, snatching Pooh's bucket. He put all four paws in at once then rapidly lost his balance, knocking himself and the bucket over in a clatter.

"Tigger!" cried Rabbit, sleepily emerging from his bedroom. "Where are your manners?"

"I don't know, Long Ears," Tigger answered cheerfully. "But I think I see them hiding under the AC, scoot over."

Once the sun finally set, everyone rolled out of Rabbit's house, feeling crabby from spending the long day hiding from the heat. Outside, they found the wood transformed.

"What are those, Mama?" asked Roo.

The hot day had turned into a warm, summer night. The grass was cool, the sky clear, and all about the trees flickered with twinkling lights.

"Fireflies," said Kanga, smiling.

Rabbit, Pooh, and Tigger grabbed blankets from the house. Soon everyone was lying in the grass, watching the lightning bugs dance. After, they stayed to listen as Rabbit, wearing his headlamp, read a bedtime story to his tomatoes.

"It was a pretty nice day after all, don't you think, Pooh?" asked Piglet as they walked home.

"Yes," said Pooh, yawning. "A very nice day."

In Which Eeyore Goes to Therapy:

SESSION 114

——〜〜〜〜〜——

EYORE WAS MAKING a gratitude list, naming things that made him happy.

"I like the little Piglet. He's my favorite size," said Eeyore. "I like Pooh Bear's kindness. I like that Rabbit always has snacks, and Kanga's warmth, and that Tigger is so bouncy. And I like that Owl sends out a newsletter to the whole wood for free."

"Eeyore!" exclaimed Dr. Festinker. "Look at all this positivity! You've made so much progress!"

"I think so, too," agreed Eeyore. "I've been feeling sunnier as of late."

"That's wonderful," beamed the skunk.

Eeyore smiled and looked out the window at the fine autumn morning in the forest. The sun dappled between green and bronze oak leaves, greeting the donkey with waving branches in the cool, fresh wind.

"Oh no," sighed Eeyore. "Looks like rain."

In Which Kanga Has
a Night Out

~~~~~~~~~~~~~~

KANGA COULDN'T REMEMBER the last time she heard her name without the addition of Roo's. It was always "Kanga and Roo this, Kanga and Roo that . . ." Kanga and Roo always.

"I used to keep books and snacks in my front pocket," sighed Kanga, rubbing the pouch on her stomach. "Now, it's just enough room to carry Roo, and no room for myself."

So when one of Rabbit's many relatives mentioned a crafting meetup for single parents in the Hundred Acre Wood, Kanga agreed to attend, even though it made her extremely nervous to meet new animals. She needed to remember what it felt like to be Roo-less.

"Who-less?" squeaked Roo.

"You-less, dear," laughed Kanga, hugging her springy son. "But just for tonight."

So that night, after bath time, Piglet arrived at 7 o'clock sharp to babysit.

"Watch me jump," squeaked Roo. He promptly tripped on his pajamas and fell onto one of the eight pillows Piglet had hastily placed around the room for safety.

"Don't worry about a thing!" said Piglet as Kanga made her way out the door. "I may only be a little taller than Roo, but I brought my step stool in case we need anything on the high shelf."

❧ ❧

The crafting group met once a month by the picnic tree, a large oak north of the sandy pits where Roo liked to play. "I only have to stay for a half hour, an hour at most,"

whispered Kanga encouragingly to herself as she made her way to the meeting spot.

Sitting around a large stump were a heron, a marmot, a green woodpecker, a pine marten, and a rather grand-looking badger in a tufted hat. The pine marten, a friendly mammal wearing sensible shoes, was laying out glasses and long leaves of charcuterie around the table.

Kanga could feel nerves churning knots in her stomach as she stared at the unfamiliar animals. Unsure of how to approach, she stood awkwardly under the tree until they waved her over.

"Hello! You must be Kanga," welcomed the marten. "I'm Fern, and we're so glad you could join us for our little get-together."

"I'm a little late," apologized Kanga.

"No one's late! Except me, of course. I'm Pecky," flitted the flustered woodpecker, scrambling with a basket of knitting. She had five eggs carefully strapped in a sling around her chest. "Henry's supposed to take the night shift, but you know how it is when 'something comes up.' I couldn't find a sitter on such short notice, and if one of these gets cold—well, I don't even want to think of it."

"I thought we agreed," exhaled the badger in a husky manner. "No children."

"I suppose I'm going to leave them all by themselves?" snapped Pecky.

"Who are they going to bother? They're eggs," squawked Karen the Heron as she pulled a tote bag of magazines and decoupaging tools from under her wing. "Don't mind her, Pecky. We're parents, we understand."

"We aren't all parents," murmured the badger into her glass as she took a sip.

"Caretakin' counts! Caretakin' counts!" yelled the lady marmot, slamming her wooden umbrella against the stump for emphasis. "My Uncle Fergus takes up just as much of my time as the wee'uns do ye! I won't have it, Agatha!"

"Of course Fergus counts, Fiona," soothed Fern, who had clearly organized the event. "Agatha, play nice or we won't invite you anymore."

"So," asked Kanga softly. She felt a little intimidated by such strong personalities. "What is it that you're all making?"

"I'm doin' watercolors," hummed Fiona after shooting a dirty glare at the badger. "Mind you, I'm not very good."

"It's not about being good or bad," reminded Fern. "It's about making things and spending time with one another. I'm crocheting a terrible new hat."

"I'm sure it's not terrible," smiled Kanga.

"And I?" Said Agatha haughtily as she poured herself a second glass of brambleberry wine. "I create an *atmosphere*."

Karen snorted through her long beak.

"Agatha, I think you'd get along very well with my donkey friend," chuckled Kanga.

"Then don't introduce us," sighed Agatha dramatically. "I'm hardly in the market for new friends."

Kanga pulled a sewing kit from her pouch and began embroidering her old denim shirt with daisies. She surprised herself by deciding to stay after an hour went by, then another. Plates of berries and nuts circulated the table in between thick slices of frosted carrot cake. Cups of carbonated sap water and wine were filled and refilled. As the sun set, Fiona and Fern lit candles that brought a cozy, helpful glow to their crafting and snacking.

Kanga usually felt more comfortable on her own, focusing on her inner thoughts and ideas, but that night she enjoyed listening to the others chatter around her. She tuned in and out of the conversations, offering a quick comment or joke whenever she felt up to it.

"I'm glad to see you making something for yourself," cheered Pecky. "The first few times here, most of us kept making things for our children."

"Not just children!" insisted Fiona, splashing her paints with indignation. "Some of us made them for difficult elderly family members!"

"Hush, no one's slighting you or your mad uncle," chided Karen.

"Is that alright?" said Kanga, thinking maybe she should've brought that quilt for Roo she hadn't yet finished.

"Of course!" said Fern warmly. "You need to make things just for you, things you'll enjoy. You've got to make time to do special things for yourself."

"That's what I always say," drawled Agatha.

⸎ ⸙

The moon was high in the sky by the time Kanga bounced her way home, promising to bring her specialty violet loaf to the next craft gathering. In no time at all she arrived back home to find an exhausted Piglet wiggling off her couch.

Her place was roughly tidied up from what appeared to be a trying evening.

"Roo was good! Except he wouldn't sleep," explained Piglet. "So we tried jumping rope, then jumping pillows, then jumping Piglet—that's when he jumps over me while I lie down on the floor, too exhausted to move. I <u>still</u> couldn't get him to lie down. Finally, I called Owl over to tell Roo a bedtime story . . . he's been asleep ever since."

"Owl's helpful that way," smiled Kanga, who had invited Owl over herself many nights when Roo wouldn't lie down. "Piglet, would you mind watching Roo again next week or so?"

"Not at all!" squeaked Piglet. "I'd be happy to come by anytime—that is, if you don't mind if I ask Owl or Pooh to help get Roo's bounces out."

So it came to pass that every other week or so, Roo would spend an evening with his great friend Piglet, and if he was feeling particularly bouncy, with Owl and Pooh as well. On those nights, Kanga would go to spend time with her new friends at the crafting circle. Or, if she was feeling burnt out from socializing, she would relax in the grass and enjoy spending time alone.

"After all," said Kanga to herself. "Roo-with or Roo-less, I am excellent company."

In Which Piglet
Downsizes His Home

~~~~~~~~~~~~~

O NE FINE SPRING morning, Piglet stood in
the middle of his house, anxiously surveying his
belongings.

"There's no reason for such a small animal to have so very
many things," squeaked Piglet, disappointed in himself.

So Piglet carefully held each object he owned and asked
himself if it "ignites delight." (Or was it "his key to glee"?
"Feel kissed with bliss?" Owl had lent him a book about
tidying up, but Piglet had lost it in the mess.) Then, he

placed each item into one of three tidy piles in the center of the room:

One pile was for items he wanted to keep.

One pile was for items he could give as presents.

And one pile was for items to donate.

In the "To Keep" pile was a stuffed carrot (a birthday gift from Rabbit), his prized collection of haycorns, and his electric toothbrush, which was now more of a regular toothbrush since Piglet had lost the charger.

In the "To Give as Presents" pile, Piglet had many useful items, including a pair of fine gardening trowels for Rabbit and a yoga mat printed with the phrase *NAMA-STY* that would be very nice for Roo. "After all," reasoned Piglet, "a yoga mat is for exercise, and Roo is always jumping and bouncing around. I only use it as a picnic blanket, which is not very athletic at all."

The biggest, by far, was the "To Donate" pile. Stacked higher than Piglet's head was a heap of odds and ends: old wrapping paper, a spare teapot, two commemorative T-shirts from the "Pooh Sticks for the Fix" fundraiser they'd held last

year to raise money to rebuild Eeyore's home, a homemade tea cozy, one red balloon, a dusty umbrella, and a game of Hungry Hungry Heffalumps, in which the Heffalumps were no longer hungry.

As Piglet marveled at the enormous mound of junk—that is to say, objects to be donated—he realized he had no idea how to get rid of it. Heffa and Ronald, the Heffalump and Woozle who managed the wood's only recycling and reuse center, were away on holiday visiting Heffa's family in India and would not be back for another month.

"Oh, oh, what now? What do I do?" trembled Piglet, who felt very uncomfortable leaving a messy heap in the middle of his house. After all that work gathering and sorting his belongings, his home was no less cluttered than it had been when he began—in fact it was even messier! That seemed rather unfair to Piglet.

He spied his closet, newly empty after all of the morning's efforts.

"Such a shame to leave a closet empty," said Piglet, "when a closet loves to be full."

So, with great strain, Piglet slid the donation pile across the floor. Heaving and shoving with as much strength as his little muscles could muster, he pushed the entire heap through the narrow closet door. Then Piglet quickly closed the door and latched it.

"There," said Piglet.

He placed the items in the "To Keep" pile on his shelf and, after much dithering, decided to hide the "To Give as Presents" pile under a tablecloth until he had a better idea of where to put them.

"Much cleaner," beamed Piglet, satisfied.

Feeling very proud of himself, he celebrated by taking a walk with his good friend Pooh, during which he found three new haycorns to add to his collection.

And Now:
Eeyore's Guided Meditation
for Gloomy Days

~~~~~~~~~~~~~~~

Close your eyes.

Take a deep breath.

With every inhale, I say, "Thanks for noticin' me."

With every exhale, I say, "It's only Eeyore, so it doesn't count."

I try to keep my breathing at this slow pace, but not too slow. Otherwise, I start to feel woozy and fall over.

When I have a negative thought, I acknowledge that I feel this way. When another negative thought comes around, I say with feeling, "I might have known you'd be back."

I acknowledge that these thoughts do not help me, but still, can't complain.

I acknowledge that sometimes I am negative, but it's better than being nothin' at all.

When I have feelings of anxiety, I say, "There is nothing
  for you to worry about right now, except for everything.
  But you can't do anything about that, so all there is to
  do at this moment is breathe."
And if that doesn't help, there's a patch of thistles to
  stress–eat.

Every single day, I become more aware of all the good
  things going on in my community, and in the world
  around me. When I feel that darkness is surrounding me,
  I know that it's only because the sky is falling, like I
  always knew it would.

Repeat after me:
Each day, in every way, things get better and better,
  as long as they don't get worse.

I know that in order to make great changes, I must challenge
  my thoughts. From this point forward, whenever I find
  myself having negative thoughts, I will immediately think
  of all the positive things in my life, and say to myself,
  "STOP . . ."

But if that doesn't work, don't blame me.
  Nobody listens to me, anyway.

In Which There Is a Bomb Cyclone (Whatever That Is)

ACCORDING TO OWL, who knew such things, the Hundred Acre Wood would soon be covered by a bomb cyclone. "Which means," huffed Owl importantly, "a powerful, rapidly intensifying storm and a sudden drop in atmospheric pressure."

"A who?" blinked Pooh.

"Is that like a—a blizzard?" squeaked Piglet.

"Not at all," said Owl. "But also, yes, very much so."

So it came to pass that one grey, January day turned to freezing, icy night. Pooh woke up the next morning to a frosted windowpane revealing piles and piles of snow, blowing in every which direction. "Oh good!" smacked Pooh over a hastily arranged breakfast of toast fingers, honey, and hot chocolate. "Time for the first snowy walk of the season with my friends."

Pooh threw on his coat, hat, and boots, took two steps out of his front door, and was immediately pushed by a gust of wind into a pile of snow. He sniffed, shaking the snow out of his ears.

This wasn't the gentle, gradual snowfall of sledding and snowy wanders that Pooh was used to.

Pooh tried to catch snowflakes on his tongue, only this snow was so blustery that it was hard to tell which landed where. "Oh, bother," said Pooh to the snowflakes. "There's so many of you, and only one of me. Perhaps you could go one at a time, if you please?"

The snowflakes responded by clumping together and landed squarely on his nose.

"I suppose we're all just excited about winter," said Pooh happily. "The more the merrier!" And, after turning back to wrap extra scarves around his chubby neck, Pooh placed a spare wool hat on his head and stumped off towards Piglet's house.

❧ ☙

As Pooh passed through the great evergreens that led up to Piglet's place, he slowed to a halt. There, on Piglet's front step, was a very small, very round sort of creature brushing away the snow in front of Piglet's house. The snow was falling more quickly than he could sweep.

"Hullo," called Pooh as he approached.

The small, round creature hopped a surprised little hop. "Pooh Bear! Is that you?" said a muffled, startled voice.

"Yes," said Pooh to the round, rather woolly creature. "I'm Pooh. And who are you?"

"It's me, Piglet," squeaked the round thing. For Piglet was wearing every sweater he owned, turning his small, pink self into a bell-shaped woolly thing with only the rosy tips of his ears peeking out beneath his felted cap.

"Well, hello, round, fuzzy version of Piglet," greeted Pooh pleasantly. "Are you ready for our walk in the wood?"

"Oh, no Pooh," trembled Piglet, visible even under all his layers. "I'd be t-t-too scared. This snow is too ferocious and strong for a small animal like me to be out in the wood."

"But we do it every year," said Pooh, confused.

"I'm sorry, Pooh," said Piglet. "But you're welcome to come in and wait out the storm?"

"Do you have any honey?" asked Pooh.

"Not at the moment," said Piglet.

"Oh well," sighed Pooh. "I will continue my walk. Perhaps you can join later?"

"Maybe," said Piglet. There was a tinge of doubt in his voice. "If the snow lets up. But Pooh! P-p-please don't be out in this b-b-bomb for too long!"

"Don't worry, Piglet!" chuckled Pooh. "My coat is from Christopher Robin. It's a handy-bound coat filled with bound, which is to say, it is bound to protect me."

Which was not at all what Christopher Robin had said. The *hand-me-down* coat was filled with *down*, not bound, and though very warm, it was hardly bombproof or weatherproof by any definition.

But Pooh was already on his way, wading through
the snow.

❦

When Pooh reached the open meadow, a wild beast of
wind pounced upon Pooh like a thousand icy Tiggers. He
was thrown this way and that way, pushed about in each
direction. All Pooh could see was white and swirling, and
soon he grew frustrated with this disagreeable wind. Pooh,
pushed to his knees by a particularly Tigger-ish gust, crawled
towards the shelter of nearby hawthorn trees.

"Oh, wind?" he called into the gale, "Would you mind
blowing a little less, if you please?" Pooh huddled behind a
snowbank for shelter. "Or perhaps, try a new direction?"

At that moment, the wind swirled against his back,
helping Pooh up. The wind pushed Pooh from behind,
helping him bumble his way through the new snowy world of
the forest.

"Why, it was a helpful wind after all!" laughed Pooh as he
bobbed and weaved past a small spinney of larch trees. He let
the wind lead him to Rabbit's, which was very convenient as
that was his next stop.

After many knocks at Rabbit's door, a crack opened
finally, and a wisp of steaming, warm air rushed out into the
blizzard to greet Pooh's icy nose. "Hullo, Rabbit,"
said Pooh.

"Pooh! What are you doing here!" said Rabbit, peering
out at Pooh through the crack in his door.

"Why, Rabbit, it's the first snow of winter," explained
Pooh, wiping the dripping icicles that were forming on his
nose. "So I came to gather you for our walk."

"Pooh!" yelled Rabbit. "This is the storm of the century!
Of the millennium! Of the zillennium! All this snow can

make things all discomboobulated—discombobulated! You need cans of soup! You need an emergency generator! You need piles and piles of toilet paper!"

"I do?" blinked Pooh.

"Yes! Get inside, quick, right now!" pressed Rabbit.

"No, thank you, Rabbit," said Pooh pleasantly. "I feel very combobu—discobooboo- . . . I am enjoying my walk very much."

"If you were smart, Pooh," warned Rabbit. "You'd go home. It's very dangerous!"

But Pooh wasn't smart, and so was already tumbling down a snowy hill towards Tigger's place.

"Such a shame to miss out on winter," sighed Pooh.

❧ ❧

During his walk through the increasingly heavy snow, Pooh discovered many new wintery things about the Hundred Acre Wood. He especially liked the fleece-lined birdhouses Kanga and Roo put out for the neighborhood sparrows. Pooh peeked inside and found the small birds all fluffed up and huddled together, peeping at Pooh to quickly close the lid.

Finally, after a great deal of effort, Pooh arrived at Tigger's tree house. When he called out "Hullo!" Tigger immediately bounced down and landed in a pile of snow.

"Brr! Grr! Blech!" Tigger spat snow out of his mouth. "What's with all this fluffy, chilly stuff?"

"It's snow," said Pooh.

"This? No," disagreed Tigger. "Tiggers know snow. Tiggers know everything about snowflakes, and snowballs, and snowtiggers sparkling in the sun. This," Tigger paused dramatically, "is an imposter."

"I *think* it's snow," said Pooh, looking around. "Just a good deal more of it than we had last year."

"Bah! Nonsense," Tigger shivered. "I do not like this."

"But Tigger," said Pooh, confused. "I thought you said you love winter."

"Preposterous!" spluttered Tigger. "Tiggers do not like the cold. Tiggers like heat! Tiggers like sunshine, and long days, and humidity. Heat is positively what Tiggers love best."

With that, Tigger bounced up to his house and slammed his door shut. He called out his window to Pooh, "Come back when it's spring!"

Now the snow was coming down in thick, cold sheets. The wind was howling. Pooh found he was suddenly quite chilly, as well as exhausted from being pummeled by the wind. He slogged through the snow, now weighing heavily against his short little legs. He tried to sing a song to lift his spirits:

Oh, I know, tut tut
In the snow, tut tut
There I go, tut tut
Moving slow, tut tut
Ho ho! Go ahead!
Want to snuggle
In my bed!
I am freezing
I am wheezing
And I'm easing
into sneezing!

As he plowed through the field near his house, the snow changed from thick and fluffy to sharp, hard flakes. Tiny balls of ice flung through the air, a slurry of winter stinging his face and nose and nipping the tips of his ears.

"Oh, brr-brr-bother," shivered Pooh. He stopped to catch his breath, leaning on a nearby snowdrift. "Is this rain, or is it snow?"

"It's a wintry mix," answered the snowdrift glumly.

"P-p-pardon?" said Pooh, as confused as he was frozen.

The snowdrift shook and shook until the snowdrift revealed itself to be a very miserable Eeyore. His pile of sticks was completely overwhelmed by the storm, turning him and his home into a snowpile.

"Hullo, Pooh," said Eeyore. "Nice day for a walk."

"Eeyore!" exclaimed Pooh. "Hullo! Are you cold?"

"Not anymore," said Eeyore. "Way past cold. Thinking of taking a nap in this snowdrift."

"A nap sounds nice," shivered Pooh.

"Of course," said Eeyore. "It's a lot warmer at your place than mine."

Pooh blinked. "Eeyore, would you like to come over to my house?"

"If it's not too much trouble," nodded Eeyore.

Leaning on each other for warmth, Pooh and Eeyore huddled out of the field and in a short time found their way to Pooh's house. Soon, they were settled under blankets in front of a roaring fire, drinking cups of malted hot chocolate with extra marshmallows.

Outside, the snowstorm slowed to a lazy, soothing pace. All over the wood white snow reflected the dazzling moon, turning the whole world to silver.

Pooh and Eeyore were fast asleep.

In Which Pooh and Piglet Do Nothing, Which Is to Say, Everything

~~~~~~~~~~

OOH AND PIGLET walked together in the golden evening, watching the shadows grow longer and longer between the trees they knew so well, and yet were always changing. For a time the pair was quiet.

"Pooh," asked Piglet. "What do you think about when you go to sleep at night?"

"I think about breakfast," said Pooh.

"And when you wake up?"

"I'm excited to eat breakfast," said Pooh. "And what about you, Piglet?"

Piglet shook his very small head. "I think of all the things I must get done that day, then I hide under the covers until I have to get up."

"Perhaps," Pooh said slowly. "You should try to think of . . . nothing."

"Nothing?" said Piglet.

"Nothing," said Pooh, nodding thoughtfully.

"It is very hard for me to think of nothing," said Piglet, trembling at the hugeness of this idea. "How do you do it?"

"Why, it's easy, Piglet," said Pooh. "I'm thinking of nothing right now."

"Then what are you doing?" asked Piglet.

"I'm listening," said Pooh.

So they listened together to noises of the forest, noticing as it moved and changed all around them. They listened and paid close attention, feeling love for that special place and each other, all the way home.

Acknowledgments

———∿∿∿∿∿———

THANK YOU TO my agent Laura Mazer, who championed this idea (and me), and to my editor Randall Lotowycz at Running Press for helping me bring this book to life. Thanks to Ellie Hajdu for teaming up with me again, to Amanda Lehr, Maeve Dunigan, and Sarah Garfinkel for your expert eyes and feedback, to Anna Cunningham for saying she wanted to read this book when I didn't think anyone would, and to Johnathan Appel for support, cheers, and pet photos.

Special thanks to St. Nell's Humor Writing Residency for giving me a place to write, and to Emily Flake for creating a space for humor writers to work.

To my fantastic sister, Molly, her partner Dan, and my loving parents, Lisa and Mark. To my cat, Catthew, for being so fuzzy. To my community of writers in Brooklyn, who are inspiringly cool and scrappy. Last but not least, to Matt, the most Pooh-ish person I know, for always keeping our home filled with snacks.

About the Author

——〰〰〰〰——

JENNIE EGERDIE is a Canadian writer and performer living in Brooklyn, NY. A contributor to *The New Yorker* and *McSweeney's,* her first book *Frog and Toad are Doing Their Best* was named one of *Vulture*'s best humor books of 2021. For more stories and humor, visit www.jennie.fun.

About the Illustrator

——〰〰〰〰——

ELLIE HAJDU is a book illustrator and a toy designer living in the San Francisco Bay Area. Her work has been featured on *Saturday Night Live, Late Night with Seth Myers,* and *Conan.* Visit her at elliehajdu.com and @elliehajdu